The Spirit-Filled Guide
to
Personal Prophecy

Lee Ann Rubsam

Full Gospel Family Publications
Appleton, Wisconsin

The Spirit-Filled Guide to Personal Prophecy

Lee Ann Rubsam

Published by Full Gospel Family Publications

All Bible quotes, unless otherwise indicated, are from The Modernized KJV.

Scripture quotations marked (ESV) are from the ESV Bible (The Holy Bible, English Standard Version), copyright © 2001 by Crossway, a publishing ministry of Good News Publishers. Used by permission. All rights reserved.

Scripture quotations marked (NKJV) are taken from the New King James Version. Copyright © 1982 by Thomas Nelson. Used by permission. All rights reserved.

Cover Photo: Lit Match, by Jeff Turner (flickr.com/photos/respres), licensed under CC by 2.0. Dimension modifications applied.

Full Gospel Family Publications
419 East Taft Avenue
Appleton, Wisconsin 54915
(920) 734-6693

Table of Contents

Introduction

In 1 Corinthians 12:8-10, the apostle Paul listed nine manifestations, or gifts, of the Holy Spirit, which were meant to occur regularly and with power in the Church. Over the many centuries which followed, as the Church became corrupted with unbelief and compromise, these manifestations were not seen nearly as much as they had been at the beginning. Fortunately, the Lord began to bring them to the forefront once again in the twentieth century. Prophecy is among them, and one of the ways it is showing up quite frequently today is in personal prophetic words for individuals.

Personal prophecy can and should be a great blessing from the Lord to His Church. It can also be an effective evangelism tool, when used rightly. But, as with any of the gifts of the Spirit, it must be cherished and guarded carefully. Because we are human and therefore open to error, there is always the opportunity for misuse and even for a counterfeit copy to show up. Those of us who are releasing prophecy to others must watch over the attitudes of our own hearts, so that our words are genuine and pure. And those of us who are on the receiving end of a prophetic word must use wisdom in discerning whether it is truly from the Lord or not, as well as maturity in how we respond to it. If we don't, we will end up disappointed, disillusioned, and perhaps stuck in the middle of big mistakes which we wish we had never made.

In this book, I will give some tips for how to discern personal prophetic words which you receive from others and what to do with those words once you've got them. I will also give some guidelines for how to keep out of trouble when you are prophesying personal words. I hope you will enjoy our journey together!

Receiving a Prophetic Word

Discerning Personal Prophecy

Discernment is a necessary spiritual skill for all Christians, if we are to successfully fulfill the unique mission which God endows each of us with. We need it at many levels to navigate the world we live in and to walk out our lives effectively for Jesus. Discernment is a component of wisdom, and there is no quick method to gain it. It comes through staying intimately connected with the Lord through prayer and reading the Bible. That said, there are guidelines which we can utilize to help us discern correctly, and in this book, we will look specifically at those which pertain to personal prophecy.

First of all, let me say that I am concerned about the emphasis which some believers put on receiving personal prophetic words from others. There are many today who run here and there to receive a word from the Lord from somebody else, when what they should be doing is spending time in the Lord's presence, listening for Him to speak directly to them.

A few years ago, the Lord shared with me a thought which really blessed my heart. My pastor had been preaching from Matthew 16:17-19, the "upon this rock I will build My church" passage. In it, Jesus speaks a personal word to Peter. My pastor commented, "What would that be like, to have Jesus Himself prophesy over you?" And the Lord dropped into my spirit that Jesus does just that on a regular basis for His children. Whenever we receive His guidance for everyday decisions, or a glimpse into His purposes for our future, or a comforting assurance that everything will be all right, He is prophesying to us personally. I am thrilled that this is the case!

What are the reasons, then, for constantly looking to others for personal revelation, rather than cultivating hearing from the Lord for ourselves? We may entertain a feeling of unworthiness to hear God. We might believe that God has special favorites whom He is eager to talk with, but think, "I am not one of them." Such ideas are really lies implanted in us by Satan. He preys upon our insecurities and feeds us ideas which sound logical, but are not true. When we agree in our minds with these falsehoods, they can create fear within us of either not being able to hear the Lord at all or of hearing inaccurately.

Another reason is fear of what God might say if He did speak to us. If we are harboring sin of any sort deep down inside, including unforgiveness, we may already have an uneasy feeling, which is really the Holy Spirit trying to get our attention. But if we're not willing to deal with our issues, it is much more comfortable to tune out His voice and only listen to whatever positive things some prophetic person is willing to share with us. (And if what is prophesied is not what we want to hear, we can always "discern" that it wasn't the Lord speaking after all!)

Still another common reason for not hearing directly from the Lord is laziness – simply not being willing to take the time to patiently wait upon God. Frankly, it is just easier to ask someone else to do our listening for us!

Some of us have an unhealthy desire to know every facet of God's plan for us ahead of time, because we would rather have it all clearly laid out before us than to have to depend on the Lord to lead us forward step by step. This is an issue of having trouble trusting God to care for us. It is also an issue of desiring to control things ourselves.

Probably most of us struggle to some extent with wanting to look into our future more than is good for us. When God is silent on the timing and details of His plan, the temptation is to see if someone else can tell us the future through a prophetic word.

So, many of us flit from conference to conference, hoping to get a knock-your-socks-off word from a national prophet. Or, we call a prophet's hotline for a personal prophecy, perhaps even slapping down $20.00 or more to the person on the other end before receiving it (which appears to me uncomfortably akin to consulting a psychic). Maybe we run from one prophetic person to another in our own acquaintance, looking for that special word which will make life all better again. One of the latest trends seems to be joining prophetic groups on social media sites, where the members give and receive revelation for one another. I can't think of a worse way to attempt to receive God's counsel than that, as there is little way of knowing for sure who most of these people are and what they might be into.

Let's get back to hearing the Lord for ourselves before we go running to others. The way to begin is by giving Him our full listening attention in prayer. He wants to speak to each of us personally. Whether He chooses to speak or not, we honor Him by making ourselves available to Him. Eventually, even if He is silent at first, we will come to understand His heart and dwell in His counsel.

I used to be one of those people who believed the lie about being outside the circle of God's special favorites. I had a hard time believing that God would want to speak to me as much as He spoke to other people, and an even harder time being confident that what I did hear was truly from the Lord. It was a miserable place to live! But one day, the Lord said quite clearly to me, *"You do hear Me well, and you need to stop second-guessing yourself."* He then directed me to John 10, the story of the Good Shepherd, and as I read its verses, I suddenly realized that all believers are given the ability to discern the Lord's voice. *All.* Here are a few promises from John 10 which we can and should take hold of:

> V. 3-5 – ... *The sheep hear His voice, and He calls His own sheep by name, and leads them out. And when He puts forth His own sheep, He goes before them, and the sheep follow Him: for they know His voice. And a stranger they will not follow, but will flee from him; for they do not know the voice of strangers.*

> V. 8 – *All who ever came before Me are thieves and robbers, but the sheep did not hear them.*

> V. 27 – *My sheep hear My voice, and I know them, and they follow me.*

If you have trouble believing that God will speak directly to you, I encourage you to meditate on John 10 until it takes hold of your spirit. Learning to hear God accurately is a process, but He'll take us there if we will believe Him for it. He wants us to know His voice, and we shouldn't despair of getting there. If you need more help with the details of how God speaks, I've written a short book for you, called *Hotline to Heaven: Hearing the Voice of God.*

So, if we're supposed to hear God directly for ourselves, does that mean it is wrong to receive a personal prophecy from others? No, not at all. It just means we should set our priorities straight. Personal prophecy should be icing on the cake, not the cake in its entirety. It is a gift from God to His people, which, according to 1 Thessalonians 5:19, 20, should be neither stifled nor despised: *"Do not quench the Spirit. Do not despise prophesying."*

Should we accept everything people prophesy as a "word from the Lord" to us? If we do, we're going to end up in a mess. There are reasons people err in prophecy. It happened in the New Testament Church too, which is why the apostle Paul said concerning prophecy, *"Prove all things; hold fast that which is good"* (1 Thessalonians 5:21).

One of the most common areas of impurity in prophetic communication is in giving dates or time frames within which fulfillment of the word is supposed to happen. The date comes and goes, and with the failure comes great disappointment or disillusionment for the recipient of the word. The prophetic utterance itself may be accurate, but the timing may not be. We'll talk about this more in our chapter, *Guidelines for Moving in Personal Prophecy.*

Some folks are speaking out of their own thinking, not by the Spirit of the Lord. Most of the time, at least on a local level, they are well-meaning people who sincerely believe they are delivering God's word. They may be prophesying from a place of insecurity, desiring to be recognized and honored as a prophet, or wanting to please others. If they are, their main motive is seeking the approval of men. They may get it right sometimes, and at other times totally miss it. We need to be merciful to them, realizing they might be in the process of maturing in hearing the Lord, and they just aren't there yet. Labeling them "false prophets" could hinder them from ever growing up into the prophetic people they are really meant to be.

Occasionally, we might encounter someone who is listening to an evil spirit, thereby prophesying out of a place of darkness. This could be because he or she is participating in occult activity, because of deep spiritual wounds which have left him or her vulnerable to hearing wrong voices, or it could proceed out of a refusal to let go of sins such as unforgiveness and bitterness.

Even well-known prophets can miss the mark, for various reasons. Physical illness or exhaustion can affect how well they are tuned in to the Lord. Spiritual warfare which is being exercised against them can cause them to have difficulty in hearing God clearly in that moment. They may feel immense pressure to perform, and if nothing is coming, they might step out "in faith" and begin prophesying in the flesh, hoping that God will then take over as they speak.

In some circles, it is commonly taught that the prophet can step into prophecy at will and decree into existence whatever he deems necessary or right. They assume that because they carry the mantle of a prophet, their prophetic words will be of the Lord, simply because they are intentionally acting in their prophet role. I think that is a dangerous place to operate from, and the teaching which has fostered it is wrong. It takes more integrity than some possess to admit that they don't have anything from the Lord right then and there, or that they are unsure of what they are receiving.

In any case, it is our responsibility to discern any word given to us. Let's look at 1 Thessalonians 5:20, 21 again, this time in the ESV: *"Do not despise prophecies, but test everything; hold fast that which is good."* In addition, 1 John 4:1 exhorts, *"Beloved, do not believe every spirit, but try the spirits whether they are of God ...."* Although John was speaking specifically of false teachers or prophets who were presenting the heresy of Gnosticism, the concept of testing or trying what is said, to measure whether it lines up with God and His Word, is also valuable in discerning personal prophecy.

Whether a personal prophecy is in accordance with God's Word, the Bible, is the first question we should ask in discerning it. If it does not line up there, there is no need to even ask into it any further. But there are other questions we can apply in the proving process, and we will talk about them in the next chapter.

Criteria for Discerning a Word

In the last chapter, we talked about a few reasons why personal prophecy might not be accurate. It is our responsibility to test a word, rather than naively swallowing it without discerning it. Here are some points we should consider in the discerning process:

Does the prophetic word line up with the Bible? If it conflicts with God's Word, it needs to be thrown out. Enough said. You need not even apply the other tests.

Does it pass the edifying / exhorting / comforting test? 1 Corinthians 14:3 lays out these three: *"But he who prophesies speaks edification, and exhortation, and comfort to men"* (NKJV). The ESV words it "upbuilding, encouragement, and consolation." Exhortation can include stirring up, spurring on, or encouragement to adjust one's path, but these are all positive things. If it is a condemnatory, critical, cut-you-to-ribbons word, it's not God.

If you are receiving the word from someone who stands in the mantle of a prophet (not just someone who is prophetically gifted), exhortation could include receiving a corrective word. In Jeremiah 1:4-9, we see God commissioning Jeremiah as a prophet, and in verse 10, He tells Jeremiah what his role will include: *"to root out, and to pull down; to destroy, and to throw down; to build, and to plant."*

Notice that uprooting comes before planting, and pulling down before building. This is part of the corrective work of the prophet – but this should be done within the bounds of "speaking the truth in love" (Ephesians 4:15). God corrects His people with the ultimate intent of bringing restoration, not devastation, to their lives. Unfortunately, not all prophets are as careful as they should be with speaking in Christ-like love. You may have to get past an immature prophet's less-than-tactful delivery and still heed the correction.

"Can I have a witness?" 2 Corinthians 13:1 tells us, *"In the mouth of two or three witnesses shall every word be established."* Anytime we receive a personal prophecy, even from a well-known prophet, there should be a true witness from the Holy Spirit in our own heart as well. That can come about by:

1) Hearing the promise first in our own communication with the Lord, and then having a prophetic person speak what we have already been hearing for ourselves.

2) God speaking the message again to us personally after it is initially given by a prophet.

3) More than one prophetic person speaking the same thing to us, without the second person knowing we have already gotten that word from someone else.

4) A deep, settled knowing (or witness) in our spirit that this is right.

We should never hang all our hopes on prophetic words which we have not been hearing God affirm or reaffirm to us personally in one of these four ways. Any prophecies which do not fall into one of these categories should still be recorded and prayed into, but we should then step back and take a "we'll see" stance. They could still be from the Lord; we just need to be cautious with them and give God time to reveal whether they are authentic or not.

I was once at a gathering where several of the participants were prophesying over the rest of us. One of the ladies ministering was a personal acquaintance of mine, who was highly gifted in personal prophecy. She spoke over me that I was going to step into a new, public "platform" ministry. I had never done any public speaking, and I really had no desire to. Her word to me fit none of the four criteria I've listed here. Furthermore, I knew that she had a deep desire for public prophetic ministry herself, and could have been merely speaking over me what she personally would consider to be a blessing. So, with those points in mind, I still recorded her prophecy in my prayer journal for future reference and took the "we'll see" stance. About three years later, much to my surprise, teaching opportunities began to open up, and I remembered what my friend had prophesied to me. She had indeed been hearing from the Lord.

Does the prophetic word bring with it confusion or peace? Genuine prophecies frequently carry elements of mystery, where the meaning of what has been said is not immediately clear in all its parts. As events unfold in the future, we can look back at a prophecy and say, "Oh! So *that's* what that meant!" But they should not bring confusion, unrest, or fear into our hearts. First Corinthians 14:33 tells us that *"God is not the author of confusion, but of peace,"* and 2 Timothy 1:7 remarks, *"God has not given us the spirit of fear, but of power, and of love, and of a sound mind."*

Does it appeal to my ego? This is a biggie. We need to be wary of prophecies which tempt our flesh. Our old nature lusts for "words from the Lord" which point to glory for ourselves! Unfortunately, there are people out there who give these kinds of words on a regular basis. They are not getting them from the Holy Spirit. They are hearing them from a spirit of flattery or from a longing in their own souls to please.

In addition, sometimes spiritually sensitive people pick up on the soul-desires of a person to whom they are prophesying. If they have not learned to accurately discern between the Lord's voice and other voices, they might mistakenly perceive what they are sensing as being from the Holy Spirit. They then speak it as a "word from the Lord" about that person's destiny, "confirming" to the person things which are not part of God's plan for them at all. Unfortunately, this happens more commonly than we would like to think! It is just one more reason to seek godly pastoral counsel before contemplating a major directional change, no matter how much a prophetic word might seem to fit with your desires.

Here are some ego-stroking red flags to watch out for:

1) **Promises of great wealth:** "I see you holding millions of dollars in your hands."

2) **Promises of great influence, fame, or visible ministry:** "I see you leading crusades and ministering to tens of thousands." You immediately begin envisioning yourself as the next Billy Graham or Reinhard Bonnke (or maybe it is even prophesied over you that you will be like one of them).

3) **Promises of great authority, like unto some well-known person:** "You carry a Smith Wigglesworth / John G. Lake / Bill Johnson / Whoever-Else-Is-Famous anointing." Or worse, "You have the spirit of Smith Wigglesworth / John G. Lake / Bill Johnson resting upon you."

I think this is cause for concern. I understand what they are trying to convey — that you have a similar ministry gift or calling. But I'd much rather have someone tell me I have the Holy Spirit resting upon me for a particular ministry role, than to prophesy over me that I will have another saint's mantle. The ability to do mighty supernatural acts comes from the Lord anyway. No man has the ability to do them apart from Him. Jesus said, *"For without Me, you can do nothing"* (John 15:5).

4) **Promises of uniqueness or superiority:** "I have never encountered someone with the level of anointing you carry." Yes, God has made each of us unique, but when you are told that you will be the only one to hold a phenomenal gift or ability, or that you will have it at a level above everyone else, watch out!

5) **Promises that you will save the world in some way:** "You are going to be the father (or mother) of a national / international revival." "Your creative genius is beyond anything I have ever seen. You will invent something that will solve international problems."

The strange thing is that very few prophetic words say things like this:

~ "The Lord has designed you to serve wholeheartedly in your local church. I see nursery ministry in particular for you, and you will experience great joy in it."

~ "The Lord has called you to the ministry of helps. He's so pleased when you cheerfully do all the little things which no one else sees."

~ "The Lord has wonderful things ahead for you, but in order to get there, you must take up your cross daily and follow Jesus through much self-sacrifice."

~ "You are a forerunner – but this means you will pave the way for others. You will not see the results in your lifetime. You will lay groundwork through your faithful labor, and the harvest will come after you are with the Lord."

(Some mature prophets *do* say these things, but it seems to be rare.)

Does the prophecy produce a response in me of an awe of the Lord? Prophecies which cause soulish lusts to burn within us for recognition, power, the adoration of men, or money and other material things, are generally not coming from God. However, God can and does speak amazing things into us which are way beyond our natural talents or abilities to make them happen.

A good example is found in 1 Chronicles 17. King David desired to build a temple for the Lord. God restrained him from doing so, but then turned around and spoke to him through the prophet Nathan that He would build David a "house" – a family line of kings which would reign forever (vs. 10-15). David's response was one of humility and awe:

> And David the king came and sat before the LORD and said, "Who am I, O LORD God, and what is my house, that You have brought me to this place? And yet this was a small thing in Your eyes, O God, for You have also spoken of Your servant's house for a great while to come, and have regarded me according to the estate of a man of high degree, O LORD God.
>
> "What can David speak more to You for the honor of Your servant? For You know Your servant, O LORD. For Your servant's sake, and according to Your own heart, You have done all this greatness, in making known all these great things. O LORD, there is none like You, neither is there any God

beside You, according to all which we have heard with our ears" (vs. 16-20).

David goes on to talk more about God's greatness and His goodness to Israel. The whole tone of his reaction to the prophetic word is one of awe and dependence, and he places all of his focus back on the Lord.

If we examine a prophetic word according to these criteria, we should be able to get a pretty good idea of whether it is coming from the Holy Spirit or from the soul of man. But, what if a word genuinely seems to be from the Lord, and yet it does not come to pass? We'll talk about that in the next chapter.

Why Hasn't My Prophetic Word Happened?

What if you have been given a phenomenal prophetic word which lines up with Scripture, witnesses to your heart, is confirmed in various ways, and yet it does not happen? Was the prophecy not really from the Lord after all?

First of all, many prophecies carry conditions with them: "If you will do this, then God will do that." We can get so caught up in the promise that we skip over or forget the condition. Did God give you instruction for how to get there, and if so, did you follow through and do what He said? Or, is there an obvious process of preparation which you have acted upon? (For instance, if God has said you are going to be a financier for His Kingdom, have you attempted to learn all you can about financial matters?) God always does His part, but He expects us to do ours as well.

Most prophecies do not see fulfillment in a matter of days. Many take decades. Abraham and Sarah waited twenty-five years for Isaac. Joseph's brothers bowed down to him twenty-two years after he first dreamed about that event. Moses had revelation that he would deliver the Israelites from bondage to the Egyptians at least forty years before it happened (Acts 7:23-25).

How long it takes for fulfillment to come can depend on God threading together a series of complicated circumstances involving many people. It can also depend on how long it takes for us to mature to the place where we can handle that word finally coming to pass. God knows what He is doing, and His timing is perfect. In His love for us and for others, He makes sure circumstances work out best for all concerned. Coming into fulfillment prematurely would mean less blessing for everyone.

We can delay fulfillment of prophecy by not cooperating with the Lord, by trying to take matters into our own hands, by refusing to work with others in the local church, and by not heeding correction from the Lord or those He has placed over us as pastors.

If you see that you have already blown it in one of these areas, however, don't despair! Ask the Lord to forgive you, and offer yourself afresh to Him. Ask Him to put you back on track. Generally speaking, our mess-ups can and will cause delays, but they don't negate the word we received. God knew all along what you would do that would get in the way, but He committed Himself to getting you through to fulfilling the purpose He had for you anyway. So, pick up and go on. Your promise is still there for you.

Here are some ways to prepare for its fulfillment:

1) **Write down the prophecy you received, so that you can remember it accurately**. As time goes on, it is easy to forget exactly what was said. Our minds have a knack for adding interpretations to the original word, which are really only our own assumptions of how it will happen. After a while, if we don't have an accurate written record, it becomes nearly impossible to distinguish between the prophecy itself and any interpretations – accurate or inaccurate – which we

may have tacked on. Writing down the word will help you keep a steady course and avoid disappointment if the working out of the prophecy doesn't follow the path you expected it to.

2) **If there are conditions to be fulfilled, be diligent to do what you were instructed to do.** You can't expect God to move on your behalf if you don't take the steps He gave you for how to get there.

3) **Bathe your prophetic word in much prayer.** Pray over it in your prayer language. Contend for it. Find Scriptures which apply, and use them to pray it through.

4) **Listen for God to give you further details as time goes on.** Most prophetic words are not all laid out in one lump. The Lord expands our understanding and vision over a period of time.

5) **Ask the Lord to pour grace over His plans for you** – to put you in the right places at the right times, to give you connections with people who can help you, and to give you specific strategies to implement the plans and ideas which He has given you.

6) **Have a servant's heart.** Serve in small opportunities which come your way, especially in the local church. God prepares us to walk out our big assignments by giving us opportunities to be faithful in doing less exciting things first. He builds integrity and humility in us in this way, so that we can handle the big stuff successfully when it finally comes.

Look at every serving opportunity which presents itself as training ground. (By the way, we should never feel we have graduated from serving in small ways. If we think that certain tasks are now beneath us, all we have graduated to is a state of pride.)

I once knew a man who was the staff accountant at a large church. In spite of his position, to my knowledge, he never took a "that's not my job" stance on serving the body. He cheerfully met the needs as he saw them, from manning the information counter, to changing a light bulb, to filling the restroom towel dispensers. His example has stuck with me for many years, and I admire him to this day for his servant's heart.

7) **Be vigilant to focus on the Promise Giver (Jesus) rather than the prophetic promise.** It is extremely easy to inadvertently slip into worshiping our promises. So, watch against idolizing your destiny.

8) **Be aware that seeing a prophetic promise fulfilled often involves a death and resurrection.** We reach the end of doing all that we can do, while circumstances may seem to make the promise no longer possible. It looks like all is lost. And then suddenly, it comes to life when we least expect it.

9) **Having done all, stand (Ephesians 6:13).** When you've done your part, from being faithful to conditions, to serving, to letting God build your character, to praying it all through, it is time to declare your trust in the Lord that He will surely do it, and then determine to rest in that hope. It's up to Him now.

If we follow through on these nine points, the Lord will see to it that every true prophetic word comes through to completion. He is a pure and holy God, Who never violates His own perfect integrity.

Delivering Personal
Prophetic Words

Getting Started in Personal Prophecy

It's a good thing to desire to move in personal prophecy. The apostle Paul exhorts us, *"Pursue love, and earnestly desire spiritual gifts, but especially that you may prophesy"* (1 Corinthians 14:1). In that same chapter, he says, *"For you may **all** prophesy one by one, that all may learn, and all may be comforted"* (v. 31), and, *"Wherefore, brethren, **covet** to prophesy ..."* (v. 39). Not all of us will wear the prophet's mantle, but since the outpouring of the Holy Spirit at Pentecost, all of us who are filled with the Spirit can be used by God to prophesy from time to time. And there are ways we can increase in this gift.

Our purpose in desiring to prophesy must always be to obey God and bless others, not because of ambition for personal honor, influence, recognition, or material gain for ourselves. Paul says, in 1 Corinthians 12:7, that *"to each is given the manifestation of the Spirit for the common good"* (ESV). The temptation to deviate from this purpose of loving and blessing others into motives which are about ourselves is ever with us, because as long as we exist in our mortal bodies, we deal with needing to continually crucify our soulish appetites. Our old nature is still with us. We are supposed to subdue it and rule over it, but we must keep a watchful heart, so that it does not creep back into its old hold over us.

Our ability to move purely in personal prophecy depends on staying in close communion with the Holy Spirit. If we do that, we will prophesy well, and we will be a means through which God can demonstrate His love in the earth. There are no newly discovered methods and no shortcuts to staying in communion with Him. The old standards are still the keys – consistent habits of prayer, reverent reading of and meditating on His Word, and prayer in the Spirit (praying in tongues). Pursuing ongoing intimacy with the Lord gives us sensitive ears to hear His voice for ourselves and others. The sensitivity we develop toward the Spirit's voice makes it easier for Him to reveal to us when we have begun to veer off into self-glorification, so that we can quickly repent and shift our focus back onto honoring Him.

Here are some practical steps to help you move into the realm of delivering prophetic words:

1) **Start with a desire for greater intimacy with the Lord Himself.** We can't minister well to others unless we are willing to first attend to the Lord through spending time with Him. We also must allow Him to minister to us. If you want to prophesy to others, you must learn under the Master's tutelage by letting Him personally prophesy to you! (That is, in essence, what He is doing when He speaks to you.) Devoted time alone with Jesus is the gateway to carrying His message; it opens the way to prophecy.

2) **Ask the Lord for increased revelation knowledge and the ability to prophesy.** James 4:2 says, *"You do not have, because you do not ask."* God has already told us to desire spiritual gifts, especially prophecy (1 Corinthians 14:1, 39). He wants us to persistently ask, so that we might receive.

3) **Make yourself available to the Lord.** Say things to Him such as, "Lord, are there people I can be a blessing to today? Point them out to me and show me what to do or how to speak to them." If you are open to the Lord

working through you, He will, and one of the ways He might do it is through prophetic gifts, such as a word of knowledge, a word of wisdom, or a prophecy.

4) **Begin to step out on the promptings the Lord gives to you.** Listen for insights He may give to you about people. You might suddenly have a knowing inside about a gift or ability which God has given to a particular person. You can then use that information to encourage him or her.

Once you start speaking, the Lord may enlarge upon what you initially received. Often, He begins by giving just a word or two, a phrase, or a snapshot picture in your mind. But as you are faithful to share what you have, what starts as a trickle of revelation can widen out into a stream, whether you are giving a direct word of prophecy or simply praying prophetically for someone.

Let's Practice!

Perhaps you are still unsure how to begin prophesying. Even if you do feel the Lord prompting you, you may feel far too timid to try it out in a public setting the first few times. There's a nonthreatening way to practice until you get more comfortable with the prophetic gifts. I teach people how to do this in our *Growing in the Prophetic* seminars. I always say, if I can do it, anybody can! And people are usually pleasantly surprised to find out how easy it is. Here's how we do it:

1) Gather a few friends together who are willing to experiment with releasing prophecy to one another. Four to eight people works well.

2) Be seated in a circle, so that you can see each other's faces.

3) Choose one from the group to be the receiver of prophecy.

4) Everyone else should take a moment to ask the Lord for a picture, a word or word phrase, or some kind of impression about him or her. (I like to keep my eyes on the person as I am asking the Lord for a word for him. That helps me to stay focused.)

5) The Lord will begin to show you little things about the person you will be prophesying to, which will be encouraging. Most of what you will hear or see will be about qualities and giftings which the Lord has already given to this person. This kind of revelation is one way the "word of knowledge" (1 Corinthians 12:8) manifests.

6) Tell the person what word or phrase you are hearing, or what picture you are seeing. You might ask, "Does that mean anything to you?" If it does, great! If it doesn't, don't worry about it. It may come to mean more as the others give their prophetic input, but if it doesn't, it's OK. This is just a practice session. Nobody dies if you get something wrong.

7) After one person has shared a piece or two of revelation, the others should share theirs. You may not initially feel like you have anything to share, but as the others do, something will click within you, and you will either find that people are confirming little promptings which you had also received, but weren't sure were really from God, or else you will find additional revelation suddenly coming to you, which fits with what the others say. Often, the individual bits of revelation do not seem all that significant, but they add up, until, like puzzle pieces, together they form a bigger picture of what God wants to say.

8) After everyone has had a chance to speak prophetically, switch to a different person in the group being on the receiving end. Begin the process again, and continue until everyone gets a chance to both prophesy and be prophesied to.

Other points to keep in mind during your practice session:

1) If the person to whom you are prophesying is someone you know well, be careful not to share as a "word of knowledge" something you would know without God's help. Expect God to give you something which you didn't think up on your own.

2) Make sure to keep what you say encouraging. "I see that you have a bitterness issue" is not appropriate in this setting! *"He who prophesies speaks to men for edification* [building up], *and exhortation* [encouragement; spurring on], *and comfort,"* according to 1 Corinthians 14:3.

3) You are not going to be receiving futuristic or directional words which are going to dramatically change someone's life, such as, "God is saying to sell all your goods and move to the jungle to do missionary work." You are participating in a fairly low level of prophetic revelation training, and it's highly unlikely that God is going to drop a whammy like that in a practice session of this type.

4) Since you aren't going to be receiving such dramatic revelation, there is no big responsibility on your shoulders. Relax and be willing to give it a shot. If you miss the target, give yourself grace, and try again.

5) Don't get hung up on whether you are giving a prophetic (futuristic) word, a word of knowledge

(speaking to the past or the present), or a word of wisdom (providing counsel or application to solve a problem). Spiritual gifts, especially the revelatory gifts, often blend and work together, and it is very common to be moving in more than one at the same time. It is not necessary to pinpoint which gift you are operating in. Simply speak whatever type of revelation God gives to you, without analyzing it.

Another way to practice prophecy is simply by praying with people about their needs. As you pray together, you may find that God gives you particular words, phrases, pictures in your mind, or insights, which assist you in knowing how to tackle the issue. You may also find yourself moving in the gift of discerning of spirits, as part of knowing how to pray. Praying according to what you hear in your spirit is what we call "prophetic prayer," or "flowing in the Spirit."

In Chapter 2 of her book, *The Voice of God*,[1] Cindy Jacobs comments that prophetically praying one-on-one with people is often the gateway into greater realms of the prophetic gift. In my own life, I have certainly found the avenue of prayer to be the most effortless entrance into prophetic revelation.

---

[1] Jacobs, Cindy. *The Voice of God*. Minneapolis, MN: Chosen Books, 1995. E-book file.

Guidelines for Moving in Personal Prophecy

Of course, we all want to prophesy only pure words into people's lives. If you are like me, you may have repeatedly asked the Lord to give you the accuracy of Elijah, or Samuel, or some other Old Testament prophet. It should be the desire of our hearts to hit the bull's-eye when we prophesy. It is something we grow toward.

In Old Testament times, prophets could be stoned for delivering a "Thus says the LORD" ... which was not. Many of their prophecies ended up in Scripture – the infallible, God-breathed Word of the Lord. However, we see that Elijah and Elisha oversaw schools for young prophets (2 Kings 2:3-15). Samuel seems to have done this as well. 1 Samuel 19:20 mentions a *"company of the prophets prophesying, and Samuel standing as appointed over them."* Elijah and Elisha also invested themselves in discipling a few young prophets through one-on-one training. That suggests to me that even in Old Testament times, there may have been some room for people to practice and make mistakes as they learned to prophesy. We just don't hear about what those prophets said and how they might have blown it.

There is also an interesting episode in Jeremiah's life, recorded in Jeremiah 32:6-9:

The word of the Lord came to me, saying, "Behold, Hanameel, the son of Shallum, your uncle, shall come to you, saying, 'Buy my field, which is in Anathoth, for the right of redemption is yours to buy it.'"

So Hanameel, my uncle's son, came to me in the court of the prison, according to the word of the LORD, and said to me, "I ask that you buy my field, which is in Anathoth, in the country of Benjamin: for the right of inheritance is yours, and the redemption is yours. Buy it for yourself."

Then I knew that this was the word of the LORD.

It appears that Jeremiah was not completely certain whether he had heard the Lord accurately until he saw the fulfillment play out. "*Then* I knew that this was the word of the Lord."

So, strive for accuracy in what you deliver prophetically, but if you miss it sometimes, remember that you are still growing (even if you've been doing this for a while). If you miss it, pick up and go on. And – this is important – be quick to humbly admit your mistakes. People will usually give you grace if you have an attitude of humility. But no one has much patience for someone who stubbornly refuses to admit error. God esteems a humble heart even more than man does. He will work with and greatly favor the man or woman who remains teachable.

There are some general guidelines we can follow, though, to keep ourselves from making embarrassing and trouble-causing mistakes, as we move in personal prophecy. Let's look at some basic do's and don'ts:

Stay away from pronouncing negative personal prophecies over people. There are times when people need correction, but unless you are operating pastorally or in what has sometimes been called "the office of the prophet," it's not your place to speak a correctional word. If you are a fully-functioning prophet, you're probably not reading this book for your own instruction. So, if you are reading this, you're not there yet. Pastors and prophets who are worth their salt handle correction in a thoughtful, tactful, discreet manner.

Are you going to see some negative things about people, as you step into personal prophecy? Absolutely! It goes with the territory of being sensitive in the spirit realm. But we don't have to blurt out whatever we see or sense.

The first time I was given opportunity to minister in personal prophecy, I was immediately impressed with the intense anger in the lady I was supposed to speak over. I am so glad I had the presence of mind to keep it to myself. If I had spoken what I saw, that word could have acted as a curse upon her. It would have hurt her deeply, and could have closed her heart to trusting people to prophesy over her in the future.

When we are aware of negative attributes in people, we have to understand that God sees their issues through a lens of compassion. He knows what happened to them to make them the way they are. If we will listen to the Holy Spirit and ask for His assistance, He will help us to speak kindly to their hurt with a word of hope, rather than wounding them further. He will give us words which hold the power to propel them into overcoming their challenges. He will give us revelation of what they are to become or accomplish, not what they presently are.

Be aware of your surroundings and who is listening in. If revelation – even positive revelation – is of a sensitive nature which the person you are prophesying to might not want others to be privy to, take him or her aside and deliver the message privately. It is not appropriate to cause people embarrassment or to raise needless questions about them in the minds of onlookers.

Some balance in walking this out is needed. On one hand, you don't want to divulge more in the presence of others than you should, but on the other hand, don't let fear of whether or not it is appropriate to speak paralyze you into not prophesying at all. Ask the Lord for wisdom. He is willing to assist you.

Avoid giving a concrete date for the fulfillment of a prophecy. This isn't a hard and fast rule, but you do have to use common sense. While, for the average prophetic person, saying, "By January 25 of next year, you will have the job of your dreams" would be an unwise way to prophesy, you could temper that by saying: "I believe God has an ideal job ahead for you. I sense that it might happen soon, even by the end of next January, but if it doesn't, be encouraged that God is still going to get you there."

Some experienced prophets can speak words right down to the date with great accuracy, but for most of us, it is best to avoid doing that. Dates are the most common area of erring prophetically. Missing the date or time frame does not necessarily mean the main point of the prophecy was inaccurate.

Why do dates tend to be hard to see or hear accurately? I don't think anyone knows for sure. It is possible that a date represents the ideal way the prophecy could work out, but that someone either directly or indirectly connected to the prophecy's fulfillment lags behind in doing their part. This, then, contributes to delay. Also, our minds are prone to supplying additional ideas (such as dates) which can smudge the pure prophetic word. The apostle Paul said, *"We know in part, and we prophesy in part,"* and, *"For now we see through a glass darkly* [unclearly]," indicating that our revelation is limited (1 Corinthians 13:9, 12). Whatever the reason, we must be careful with prophesying, or clinging to, a date.

Don't prophesy to Jane Smith that she will end up marrying Dan Jones. Just don't ever go there. It could stir up desires and emotions which should never be awakened in the receiver of the prophecy. It's a recipe for heartache and embarrassment. If you think you are hearing such a thing, keep it to yourself, and leave it with God. I would not even recommend praying behind the scenes for it to happen. Just be quiet and leave it with God. If at some point Jane and Dan end up married, you can smile inwardly, knowing you really did hear God, but if it doesn't happen, you can laugh at your own immaturity and be thankful no one but God knows you ever had that thought.

Don't prophesy babies. Do you think you are hearing that Sister Jeannie is going to have a baby? Keep it to yourself. A baby prophecy can cause great hope to the barren – but then extreme pain if you missed God, and it doesn't happen. Do well-seasoned prophets prophesy babies? Sometimes, and their prophecies are fulfilled. This book is not intended for prophets with that level of experience.

If Sister Jeannie asks you to pray for her to be able to have a baby, should you do that? Of course! She will appreciate your prayers, and you can believe together for God to answer. Just be careful what you say, and don't prophesy it as "the word of the Lord." Petitioning prayer, in its place, can be more effective than a word of prophecy in accomplishing a desired end such as this.

Avoid prophesying changes in direction or vision to a pastor in front of his congregation. A prophecy which concerns adjusting direction or vision for the church should always be given privately, so that the pastor and his leadership team can discern the word and decide how and when to implement it in the best way for the church.

If you think you have something directional for a pastor for his personal life, give that message privately too, so as not to awaken questions or concerns in the body. For instance, prophesying a change in location for the pastor, or a shift into a new ministry, may be completely accurate, and yet, speaking it in front of the congregation can cause fear and insecurity for the people he pastors.

Don't let someone pressure you into prophesying. If you don't have something, pray that the Lord would give you the needed word. But until He does give you something, the appropriate response is to frankly admit, "I'm sorry, but I am not hearing anything."

Don't let someone pressure you to add to a word or to interpret it beyond what you have. Sometimes you will not only hear a word, but the Lord will also give you further interpretation or application of it. At other times, you may only receive a few words, or a snapshot picture. It is important not to go beyond what you do have from the Lord into add-on guessing. If you do, most likely you will guess wrongly.

Especially if you are seeing something of a symbolic nature, it is easy to jump to conclusions about what it means. This can, and probably will, result in delivering an inaccurate interpretation. If the person you are prophesying to asks for more than you have from the Lord, it is best to simply say, "I don't know. Perhaps the Lord will give you greater understanding as you pray into it further. Maybe you will have to wait to see it unfold."

There are at least four places in the Bible in which God warns us not to add to, or take away from, what He has said. That applies to how we treat Scripture, but it is also how we should handle prophetic revelation. Proverbs 30:6 warns, *"Do not add to His words, lest He reprove you and you be exposed as a liar."* (The other references are Deuteronomy 4:2, Deuteronomy 12:32, and Revelation 22:18, 19.)

Avoid pressuring the person you are prophesying to into action. It is your place to speak forth the word, but it is not your responsibility to see it through to fulfillment. You don't need to go back to the one you prophesied over and remind him repeatedly of it.

You may deliver a true prophecy which never comes to pass, because the person receiving the word rejects it or does not fulfill conditions connected with it. That is not your problem. It is up to the receiver of the word to discern the word, whether he or she does so correctly or not.

Allow yourself the freedom and peace of heart to let go of prophetic utterances once you have spoken them. And, remember that although the word you are speaking feels like an urgent "now" word to you, it may take years to reach fulfillment. Let it rest.

When possible, have the prophecy recorded. With the proliferation of cell phones with voice recording capabilities, this is very easy to do. A recording protects you from someone accusing you of saying something which you did not. It also helps everyone involved to remember the word accurately, so as not to wrongly interpret or add to what was actually said. Make the person you are prophesying to aware that you are recording the word, or encourage him or her to record it for later reference.

Make sure you are hearing the Lord, rather than seeing into the soul of the person you are prophesying to. Prophetic people are often very sensitive in the spirit realm, and they can pick up on voices which are not necessarily the Lord's. They are also susceptible to mistaking what is in the heart of another person for being God's will for him or her.

We do damage to people's lives by prophesying over them things which are not God's plan at all, but are instead inordinate desires which they harbor inside. If we do that, we "confirm" to them what they long for, and they may then use our "word" to justify launching into something which those who know them well can see clearly is a disastrous path for them. I have personally seen this happen a few times, as have many pastors, much to their sorrow on behalf of their sheep.

How can you avoid this mistake? By listening carefully for checks in your spirit which may accompany an initial impression. Learn not to speak hastily. Take a few moments to discern before releasing a word. Resisting the urge to deliver over-the-top, ego-stroking words can also alleviate this problem. Keep it simple, and don't embellish the straight word or vision you are receiving.

Be careful not to make your prophetic words a measure of your importance or an issue of your reputation. Everyone wants to be accurate, but it is important not to put the focus on yourself. Let Jesus be the focus, along with serving others. The Lord uses prophecy as He sees fit, and the working out of a word may not look like what you envisioned, when it happens. He will take care of your reputation, if you will stop striving to vindicate it.

Paul comments in 1 Corinthians 4:7 (NKJV), *"For who makes you differ from another? And what do you have that you did not receive? Now if you did indeed receive it, why do you boast as if you had not received it?"* In other words, no matter what ministry function or supernatural gift we operate in, including prophecy, we are not doing it of ourselves. It is the Spirit moving in and through us. In addition, God gives His gifts sovereignly, not according to how spiritual we are, or how well we perform. None of it is about us, so let us glory in Him, not in ourselves.

For further ways to avoid inaccurate prophecy, please see the *Criteria for Discerning a Word* chapter. Although it is written for the person on the receiving end of a revelatory word, keeping those criteria in mind will also help you prophesy more accurately.

Beyond Church Walls

We often think of prophecy as something which is supposed to take place within the context of church gatherings — and it truly is meant to flourish there. However, as the revelatory gifts of the Spirit have begun to reemerge and be poured out in greater measure among believers in the last few decades, many are discovering their value as a vehicle to reach the lost. They are taking the prophetic to the streets.

Is this biblical? Yes. We see it primarily in the Old Testament, with the prophets releasing the word of the Lord to those who knew and revered Him, but also to kings and common folk who had no knowledge of Him or desire to follow Him. In the New Testament, Paul prophesied a declaratory word to Elymas the sorcerer that he would be blind for a season, because he tried to keep the ruling official of Cyprus from believing the gospel. The word immediately took effect upon Elymas, causing the government official to believe on Jesus (Acts 13:6-12).

Perhaps the best New Testament example of prophetic evangelism is found in John 4:1-42, the story of Jesus and the Samaritan woman at the well. She believed on Him because He spoke a word of knowledge to reveal specific details of her dysfunctional life. Not only did she believe, but *"many of the Samaritans of that city believed on Him for the woman's saying, who testified, 'He told me all that I ever did'"* (v. 39).

From a practical viewpoint, most of us have more opportunity to prophesy in everyday life than we do in the context of a few hours of church services or related church activities every week. We rub shoulders with people from Sunday through Saturday who are in desperate need of guidance and the understanding that God actually cares to give it to them. We can, through the prophetic gifts, release to them a revelation of the Father's love for them.

In 1 Corinthians 14:24, 25, Paul indicated what happens to the nonbeliever who encounters prophecy: *"But if all prophesy, and one comes in who does not believe, or is unlearned, he is convinced of all; he is judged of all. Thus are the secrets of his heart made known, and so, falling down on his face, he will worship God and report that God is truly in you."* Although Paul was giving instruction in the context of church gatherings, the principle can be applied to how nonbelievers respond to supernatural revelation outside the church walls as well.

How can we release prophetic gifts in our everyday world? Some people are using personal prophecy as a means of evangelism at New Age or Renaissance fairs. They set up booths, dispense words of knowledge and prophecy, and then present the gospel message. Some approach people on the street with an offer to speak prophetically to them as a means of bringing them to salvation. This is all wonderful, and if you are a bold person who gets excited by the potential of such ministry, or if you are already quite comfortable with operating in the revelatory gifts, a prophetic evangelism team of this type could be your place to thrive.

But, such a ministry method would be too much of a stretch for many of us, especially when we are first stepping into prophecy. So, let's look at a simpler, more natural, less intimidating way to begin:

Step one is to offer our willingness to the Lord. We can pray, *"Father, please use me to glorify Jesus wherever I go today. Help me to have a heart sensitive to the promptings of the Holy Spirit, and give me the faith to do and speak whatever He shows me. If there is someone You would have me speak prophetically to, I am available to You."*

Step two is to keep in a state of expectancy that God will answer that prayer, staying alert for the inner nudges of the Spirit. You probably won't have an opportunity present itself every day, but by staying conscious of being about your Father's business like this, you won't miss the opportunities when they do come your way.

Step three is to obey the inner promptings when you sense them. Now we get into the part that feels risky. How does one initiate the prophetic gifts in public, perhaps with total strangers, without being totally awkward? Walking up to an unfamiliar person and blurting out, "In the spirit, I see a waterfall over your head" is definitely going to sound weird. You don't want to scare people, and you don't want somebody calling for a security guard!

One of the best ways to begin in prophecy is by praying with people. Prayer is often a gateway to revelation. As you pray with others for their needs, the Holy Spirit will give you ideas, phrases, and pictures in your mind to assist you in how to pray. These are really prophetic impressions. You may not even recognize them for what they are at first, because they often come as gentle nudges. As you pray, sometimes you will also receive divine counsel or other information to further help the person for whom you are praying.

If we are going to pray with people, we first have to be willing to talk to them. Although it's possible that a stranger may strike up a conversation with you, and it's important to pay particular attention when someone does (this may be a God setup), if you wait for that to happen, your opportunities to minister in prophetic gifts may be rare. Be proactive. Take time to initiate casual conversation when that is a natural thing to do – with the person sitting next to you on an airplane, people waiting in line with you at a store checkout, wait staff at restaurants, baristas at your favorite coffee shop, etc. Stores you frequently visit may work well, because you have already built up a small bond of trust simply by being a familiar, pleasant customer.

Your workplace may provide opportunities for you to pray with people and speak into their lives prophetically, because you already have a level of relationship with your coworkers and/or customers. I realize this has become more difficult in recent decades, due to many employers prohibiting their employees from talking about the Lord, so be sure you clearly understand your company's policy. If you are self-employed, though, you have the freedom to use the openings God gives to you to release blessing into your customers and clients.

If you are a caring listener, the people you talk with will sometimes share pieces of their lives which signal that they need prayer. The Holy Spirit may also alert you to their unspoken prayer needs. Many people are weighted down with problems which they have no idea how to get relief from, and they will sometimes be open to receiving prayer, even if they don't have a personal faith in the Lord.

Use questions to probe whether people are willing to receive prayer, as well as whether your prophetic impressions are accurate: "May I pray with you for the knee pain you mentioned (your job situation, your daughter, etc.)?" If you experience a flash image of a piano in your mind, you might ask, "Do you play piano?" Or, "Are you a musical person?" A name may pop into your mind, and you can then ask, "Does the name Brian mean anything to you?"

You could end by assuring them that God cares about what they are going through, and that He wants to get involved in their lives. You might even, through on-target prayers and prophetic revelation, be able to lead them to Jesus.

Whether you are engaging in personal prophecy within the church setting or out in your everyday world, be open to letting the Holy Spirit use you in even the smallest ways. What seems of little significance to you may be huge to the person you are serving through your prophetic gift. We all need to start somewhere, and simple prayers which are led by the Spirit are a nonthreatening way to begin. Expect Him to increase the revelatory gifts within you as you are obedient to step out at His bidding.

Summing It Up

In this book, I've given you some ideas for how to avoid pitfalls in both delivering and receiving personal prophecy. By their very nature, these guidelines could make the subject seem a bit negative. And I know that my chapter on taking personal prophecy beyond church walls could be quite a stretch for some of my readers.

You might be tempted to feel overwhelmed, throw up your hands, and say, "Maybe I will just avoid all this personal prophecy stuff altogether!" Please don't do that! The Lord deeply longs to give all of His children revelation from heaven. He implants the gift of prophecy in us as a means of blessing the Church and the world around us. He only gives good gifts, which are meant to be embraced, not feared.

Even though the Corinthian believers had much immaturity to overcome in their pursuit of spiritual gifts, the apostle Paul still encouraged them to *"desire spiritual gifts, but especially that you may prophesy"* (1 Corinthians 14:1). There was a growing process involved for them, and there is one for each of us, too.

If you would like to learn more about becoming a revelatory person, I have written more extensively on the subject in my book, *The Intercessor Manual.* You might also enjoy *Growing in the Prophetic*, an audio resource taken from a seminar I teach. You can purchase either of them at my website, *Full Gospel Family Publications.* You will find additional free information on prophetic topics at my blog, *Out of the Fire.* I hope you will visit me there!

May I close by praying for you?

Dear Heavenly Father, I thank You that every good and perfect gift comes from You, including the gift of prophecy. I pray for my readers that they will grow in godly wisdom. Increase their understanding and their sensitivity to Your Spirit, and impart to them the ability to operate in the prophetic gifts, so that they can draw others closer to You. Give to each of them a discerning heart, so that they will be able to tell the difference between genuine words from You and those which are merely the thoughts of men. May they increase ever onward and upward in revelation of Your ways and of Your Son, Jesus. In Jesus' name, amen.

About the Author

Lee Ann Rubsam is a Christian author, essayist, and teacher who specializes in writing about prayer and Christian character building. Her materials are used by churches, home study groups, and home schooling families throughout the world.

One of Lee Ann's primary interests is to encourage intercessors in their calling and to help them reach their highest level of effectiveness in prayer. With that goal in mind, in addition to her books, she and her husband Paul present practical, hands-on intercessor workshops around the nation.

For other books by Lee Ann, please visit her publishing website, *FullGospelFamily.com*.

For information about hosting an intercessor workshop in your area, visit *OutOfTheFireMinistries.org*, or contact Lee Ann at leeann@leeannrubsam.com.

Other Books by Lee Ann Rubsam

Made in the USA
San Bernardino, CA
17 June 2015